↻ A view of The Lowry, iridescent in the early evening, making clear the quality of transparency reinforced both by bold colours and illumination to create a powerful effect in the surrounding water.

For

David Alston

People have talked of the renaissance in Britain's cultural building stock ushered in by the Lottery bonanza. Significantly, however, much of this has been about renovation - albeit superb - or conversion - albeit stunning - of extant buildings. When all is said and done, Tate Modern remains a converted power station - with many of its powerful massing and spatial effects orchestrated out of the shell and substance of the original building. The political will and communal confidence to build new and imaginative cultural buildings is still wanting in our present-day national make-up… with some singular exceptions. All of this makes the achievement of Salford and Michael Wilford's Lowry the more remarkable. This is a bold new build, employing challenging architecture and engineering, and has become a landmark structure in full and enjoyable use, welcoming its millionth visitor before its first birthday.

A building like The Lowry does not come about without vision and tenacity on the part of its champions. In the late 1980s, those within Salford City Council working on the long-term strategy to transform the derelict docks must be applauded for their determination to have a landmark building as a spur to regeneration. Those who subsequently honed concepts and shaped the brief for the building, arguing over practicalities, created the invaluable and essential dialogue between client and architect.

The Lowry was always going to be of major significance for Michael Wilford and Partners. At the beginning of the process he was part of the longstanding internationally

1

acclaimed partnership of Stirling Wilford. With the sad loss of James Stirling at the incipient design stage for The Lowry complex, Michael was posed with the phenomenal challenge of seeing this building through as the first truly in his own right and idiom. In the early stages until the three Lottery distribution bodies enabled the financing of the building, the architects worked speculatively. All along, the building was going to have huge practical demands, which would have to be accommodated within other more purely architectural concerns.

The Lowry that emerged from this process is a wonderfully photogenic, eighteen hour-a-day building, much talked about by its visitors and audiences, a "people-watching"

building creating a social and relaxed arena for the general public and a hard-working building with theatre spaces and galleries which actors, performers and artists have really taken to playing and exhibiting in. In 2001 the building has attracted a number of prestigious awards for its architecture including Building of the Year from the Royal Fine Art Commission Trust. Significantly the citations for such awards have emphasised the enjoyment the public are getting from being in the building.

Lowry Press invited the architectural critic Deyan Sudjic to appraise the building; the essay which follows is beautifully complemented by Richard Bryant's photographs to create a small document of a great achievement.

↻ A typically bold feature: a balcony and stair, high in the entrance foyer.

The Lowry - A Landmark
Deyan Sudjic

The Lowry has transformed Salford. It is a remarkable popular success, turning a derelict industrial backwater into a focus for the whole of Britain's North-West, attracting people not just to its diverse programme of cultural events but also to experience its rich sequence of public spaces. It has become a new kind of city centre, bringing life to a collection of redundant dockland wharves. And it represents a powerful work of architecture in its own right, serving as an authentic civic landmark.

The Lowry is the product of a broad and complex range of motivations. It was first mooted in the guise of an opera house, an heroically ambitious conception, and one that was later modified into a lyric theatre with the subsequent addition of a secondary studio theatre, a configuration judged to stand a better chance of commercial success. The complex also houses Salford's L S Lowry collection and exhibition galleries, alongside the usual collection of bars, restaurants and shops that form part of so many Lottery-funded projects, as well as ArtWorks, an interactive gallery aimed primarily at families and young people.

The Lowry is also a reflection of Salford's determination to reassert its independent identity alongside its higher-profile next-door neighbour, Manchester. It is an attempt to bring investment into the area and an expression of the City Council's cultural ambitions.

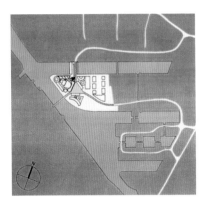

And in the end it is about creating a place that people want to be in.

The centre forms the new heart of Salford Quays, the landlocked harbour on which the whole region's prosperity was built in the late 19th and early 20th centuries, but which lost its raison d'être when changing patterns of trade left it high and dry, and made its wharves and warehouses redundant. The Lowry is a seed planted in the middle of what was dereliction, and is an enormously brave attempt by its architect, Michael Wilford, and the Lowry Trust to bring the area back to life.

The context was a demanding one. A few giant structures, of which Manchester United's 'Theatre of Dreams' is the most conspicuous, dominate the landscape but make no more than a piecemeal, mixed and largely banal contribution to the built environment of The Quays. Clearly, it is no place for shrinking violets. And Wilford, once the partner of James Stirling - perhaps the most distinguished British architect of the 20th century, is certainly not that. Like Stirling, he has a passion for the richer architectural flavours. Wilford also has a predilection for vivid colour, strong shapes and bold forms. And he has used them in abundance to give The Lowry its bravura presence.

The plan of the dock and its redevelopment, created in 1992 by Michael Wilford and James Stirling as part of the initial feasibility study.

On the left, an elevation cut through the centre line shows the theatres and foyers, and the way in which the central store feeds each theatre, creating enormous flexibility and efficiency. On the right, a cut through the northern side of The Lowry shows the basement stores and services, the dressing rooms at stage level, the staff village above and, on the upper floors, the range of top-lit art galleries.

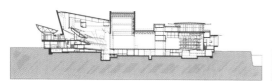

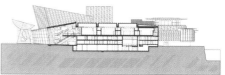

Architecture has clearly been much more than a means to an end for The Lowry. Long before funding was in place, it was the images of Michael Wilford's building that gave focus and credibility to Salford's high ambition. The architect's perspectives demonstrated that this was not just a nebulous idea, it was a real project. And it was not just a utilitarian shed, driven by expediency, it was a project that would involve a serious piece of architecture, a genuine landmark in the best sense of the word.

It is the quality of the architecture that demonstrates the scale of the transformation that Salford is determined to bring about. And above all it is the physical experience of strolling through the promenades and galleries, relaxing in the restaurants and cafés, and enjoying the sense of occasion that performances bring, that has made the building such a popular success.

Wilford's building is at heart about the fundamental, but unaccountably neglected, issue of making architectural space. It is neither architectural sculpture, nor an anonymous box inside a flashy skin. It is a building of rich complexity. As built, The Lowry is a mixture of art, drama and entertainment. The gallery spaces form a relatively modest element in what is fundamentally a theatre complex. There are two stages, one with 1760 seats, and a second, smaller auditorium with a

The interior of the Lyric Theatre showing the 'cheeks' on either side of the proscenium, which act acoustically and conceal stage lighting.

The inner and more intimate of The Lowry galleries showing the opening contemporary exhibition: 'The Double', with Thomas Ruff's *Andere Porträts* on view.

maximum of 460 seats which can be configured in various arrangements.

Despite the prestige we accord to theatres, they do not always offer promising material out of which to make architecture. For an architect trying to create a landmark, the art gallery is a much more forgiving brief than a theatre, which has to carry the weight of so much technical paraphernalia. There are too many blank walls, too many loading docks and too many escape stairs to deal with. Ultimately, the theatre runs the risk of becoming a machine designed to deliver sight lines, give the required acoustic reverberation times, move scenery and allow audiences to get in and out in safety

as fast as possible, rather than a piece of architecture, or a place for people.

But Wilford's design deals brilliantly with these potential drawbacks. He has taken the theatres, and turned them into a composition which relates to its setting by wrapping them in a continuous promenade of foyers, bars, restaurants and gallery spaces. You could come to The Lowry just to take a walk in them. Through a skilful series of changes of level that makes the main floor of the centre undulate like a gently rolling landscape, you get a series of spectacular views out over water, and find yourself moving from one space to the next, from a tight corridor to what can be interpreted

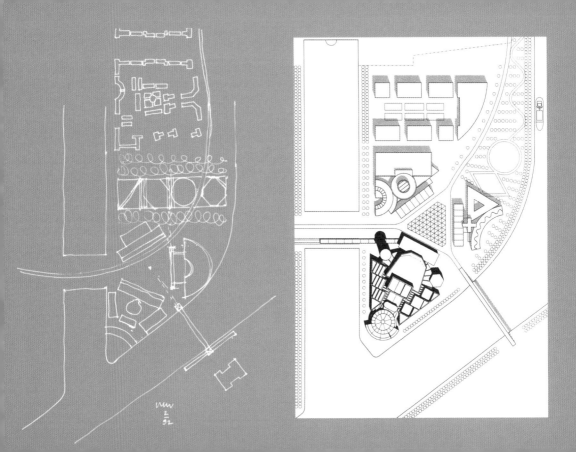

On the left is one of a series of concept sketches for the master plan of the site; the formal realisation, used for the feasibility study in 1992, is on the right.

"… to create a modern building from an assembly of archetypal architectural forms"

as a clearing in the forest, and being constantly reminded of the building itself, and of the water and sky outside.

The design did not come in a single creative move. Salford chose its architect through a series of competitive interviews. A long list of 45 who put their names forward was whittled down to six. The selectors went and looked at Stirling and Wilford's Staatsgalerie in Stuttgart and liked what they saw. The practice also had considerable experience in designing theatres and performing arts spaces. They had done a fully developed, though unbuilt design for a new opera house at Compton Verney, made an unsuccessful

competition entry for the new Glyndebourne, and built a theatre for Cornell University in Ithaca, New York.

Wilford and his partner James Stirling were commissioned to carry out a feasibility study to show how the site could be developed, and how an opera house might be fitted into it.

It was completed in the week of Stirling's untimely death in 1992, and Wilford presented the masterplan on his own. The opera house occupied much the same site that The Lowry does now, at the tip of the quay, a spit of land projecting out into the water of the basin that ships once used to turn in until the traffic finally stopped in 1982.

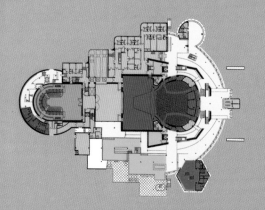

Ground Floor Plan

0 5 10 20 30

N

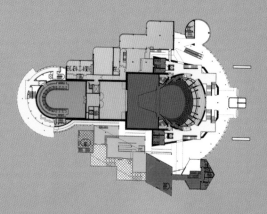

First Floor Plan

0 5 10 20 30

N

From left to right, these coloured plans of the completed building show the complicated layering and the balanced composition about the central axis. On the left is the plaza and entry level plan, to its right is the upper theatre foyers plan, then comes the galleries plan and, finally, the rehearsal room and the upper Lyric balcony plan.

Overleaf: The interior of the Quays Theatre: the colourful balconies are both dramatically suspended and cantilevered to allow an uninterrupted view of the extraordinarily variable and versatile performance space.

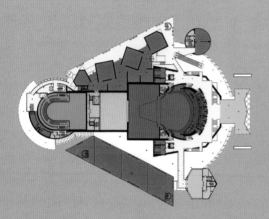

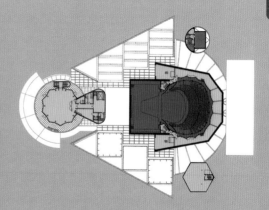

Second Floor Plan
0 5 10   20   30

Fourth Floor Plan
0 5 10   20   30

The site would have been fronted by a triangular piazza, collecting people coming in from three directions - from the new tram stop linking Salford Quays with central Manchester, from the pedestrian route established by a proposed new footbridge crossing the canal, and from the new road planned to allow visitors to drive into the area.

The masterplan proposed clustering public buildings around this piazza. As well as the Opera House, there would have been a hotel, and a planned virtual reality centre. The balance of the site would have been allocated to an office campus and a waterside park.

Salford accepted both the masterplan and Wilford's conception of the building. He proposed a dramatic composition of strong geometric forms that belongs to a sequence of designs from the practice's work. Hexagons, cylinders and cubes were seen at the built Berlin research centre (WZB), as well as the unbuilt proposals for redeveloping Kyoto railway station, Seville's stadium and the Disney Hall in Los Angeles. *"Each one is unique but there is a common strategy in our projects,"* says Wilford. *"At one time so many of our projects were not being built that ideas were drawn and redrawn, sometimes for as many as three different schemes before we actually got a chance to build them. We were always intrigued by the idea of using the*

The grand staircase of another Michael Wilford building: the British Embassy, Berlin. The stairway links the entrance of the building to the Winter Garden, and clearly demonstrates the architect's use of bold geometric forms and colour.

A view of the illuminated model of the building as built, superseding one earlier version, and showing the new form of the tower and the cladding, compared with the two drawings shown on page 19.

image of a colliery lift tower, for example. It was first mooted for a scheme we did for an office building for Olivetti at Milton Keynes. That didn't get built. But we liked it as an idea, and we tried it in another unbuilt scheme before we finally got to use it as the lift in the Stuttgart Staatsgalerie."

Something similar was at work in Wilford's design processes for Salford. The basic idea of articulating large complex buildings into assemblages of geometrically discrete identifiable smaller elements had long been one of his major philosophical starting points. Like earlier projects, The Lowry made use of this idea. And some, though not all, the elements of the family of

geometric components used in The Lowry composition had surfaced before. But familiarity was part of the point. The idea of the WZB research building in Berlin was to create a modern building from an assembly of archetypal architectural forms, a tower, a keep, an arcade and so on that could be recognised as such. The Lowry displays a similar approach, but the forms here are more abstracted. They read not so much as historically recognisably forms, but as Euclidian shapes. Perhaps these also allude to the forms of the ships that once moved down the canal.

With the plan accepted, Salford began a two-pronged strategy to realise the scheme: to assemble the funds

15

⊂ A detail of the interior showing the bold metallic signage used throughout and, again, the element of transparency.

"It reads like a castle in the desert, an oasis or a natural land form"

for The Lowry itself, and to find a commercial partner to develop the rest of Pier 8. By the time the Millennium Commission was established, and Salford had begun work on an application for funding, the Opera House had turned into the Salford Arts Centre, with a Lyric theatre and a gallery forming the core of the proposals, accompanied by an outdoor performance space. The scheme was tested by the City Council who asked potential users such as dance, opera and theatre companies to evaluate the suitability of its proposed accommodation.

The effect of that consultation was to effectively double The Lowry's size, adding a second smaller theatre and a children's gallery. And it set Wilford off on a series of

refinements that eventually resulted in The Lowry as built. The first transition had been from an Opera format to the Lyric form, established in Britain in the 19th century by Frank Matcham, and demonstrated most effectively at the Coliseum in London and the Festival Theatre in Edinburgh.

The Lyric Theatre is designed to allow for a range of uses. The auditorium and stage are big enough to accommodate opera and dance, but they are also suitable for more intimate performances, including theatre and variety. In architectural terms the opera house tends to be taller, with tiers of boxes and balconies rising vertically, and audiences being kept

Two drawings, executed in 1995 for the funding bid and showing the first plans for cladding, for the tower - which was to change both in use and appearance - and for the plaza façade, which retained the planned canopy but lost the giant video screen.

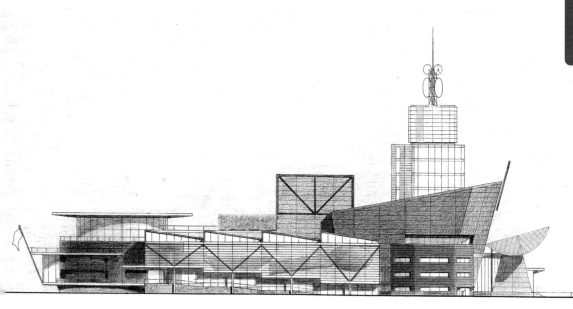

- The broad expanse of the rehearsal studio showing the streams of light and continued use of bold colour; performers enjoy excellent views on all sides as they work.
- The drawing and its realisation for the dramatic entrance foyer.

relatively remote from the performers. *"The Lyric form has deeper overlapping curved tiers of balconies. Matcham shaped the room to feel intimate and involving,"* says Michael Wilford.

"Beginning with that model, we shaped the main auditorium. It began as a perfect circle, but ended up modified into a voluptuous oval. It allows the audience to feel part of a shared experience, they can look across the auditorium to see other spectators, as well as the action on the stage."

The external impact of the changes on the building's form was to make a denser complex. In Wilford's view this too was an advantage, giving The Lowry more of a presence in its context. *"It reads like a castle in the desert, an oasis or a natural land form. I wanted it to be even closer to the water, though that turned out not to be practical, but the intensification of the brief was a benefit."* The broad outlines of the building were in place by this stage, but Wilford's working method is one of continuing refinement. As an architect, he is not afraid to change his mind when he can see the chance of getting more out of a particular element, or modify the overall composition to make it work better. Perhaps the most dramatic example of this process was over the issue of colour and external cladding materials. Wilford's original conception proposed a strongly coloured

21

C A detail of the interlocking stainless steel exterior cladding system; the effects of the light at all times of day both unifies and emphasises the bold forms of the building.

"The colour was switched from the outside to the inside"

structure. He had thought about purple, applied to the exterior of The Lowry in a skin of coloured metal panels. But with funding approval for the project already secured, Wilford began to think again about how The Lowry would look on dull days when there was no sun, or in the rain, and at night. It was then that the idea of substituting a shiny skin and moving the colour inside occurred to him. *"I decided it would be much more effective to use reflective stainless steel and glass walls. It would give the building an aesthetic unity, and provide a surface which reflects the sky and the water. It has a chameleon quality that makes it feel good on even the dullest days. At night you can even project images onto it with a regular slide projector.*

"It was one of those flashes of insight. I said, 'Let's change it,' and after I had explained exactly why, the Lowry Trust readily agreed." Bright colour did not vanish altogether from The Lowry. *"The colour was switched from the outside to the inside. The colours are used to demonstrate layering from the exterior and are designed to make it jolly and unusual. The interior glimpsed from outside is like looking into a volcano's heart, you see all the layers of colour, intensifying to white-hot yellow at the core of the building."*

There were other, compositional changes too. The tower that is such a strong element in the design, and which is now used to house the Lowry archive,

23

⟳ Left and right, these photographs emphasise the importance of the tower as a
⟴ symbol of the building. At some point it may be possible to adorn the tower at its
top with illuminated signs announcing current productions.

⟴ Overleaf Some of the colour studies for the Lyric and Quays Theatres;
this exploration of the purposeful use of colour in interiors is characteristic
of Michael Wilford's work.

was originally conceived of as accommodating the administrative staff for the gallery. This would have separated staff working in the theatres from those involved with the galleries, which on reflection was seen to be a disadvantage, and the staff accommodation was reconfigured to group both teams together. Wilford redesigned the scheme to deal with this, but it left the tower without a function. *"Some people simply wanted to remove the tower altogether, but I thought it was an important element in the composition. It reads as a beacon, visible – for the time being at least – from the motorway. So I suggested using it to provide the curatorial storage and workshop space for the Lowry collection."* The idea was accepted,

and the tower stands as a symbolic celebration of the collection, six floors high. *"It was originally going to be completely clad in solid panels from top to bottom, but we cut it back in spiralling slits, to emphasise the vortex form, and to hint at what is happening inside."*

The process of refining the design was one of give and take, some ideas coming from the architect, others from his client. *"The promenade originally went only two-thirds of the way around the building,"* says Wilford. *"The Quays Theatre foyer was an appendage, and the galleries were divorced from the water. And the Chief Executive, Stephen Hetherington, said he was disappointed that the route round the building was*

25

entirely internal. 'Why can't I see water?' he asked me." Wilford redesigned the circulation route, and repositioned the galleries to create a much more memorable experience of moving around the building.

At other times, Wilford made suggestions for improvements to the brief, arguing successfully for example for the provision of natural light to the galleries. *"You can always black them out if you need to, but you can't put back daylight if you haven't included roof lighting in the first place."*

Other design decisions were the product of more complex interactions. The number of seats in the main

auditorium was the result of a compromise. The Trust wanted to have as many seats as possible to maximise potential revenue. The Arts Council said that 1800 seats was too big for a viable theatre. The outcome was an auditorium with a degree of flexibility, both in terms of its acoustics and its seat configuration. *"I didn't like the idea of a mechanical solution that might work for the first three months, and then rusts up.*

"We have designed the auditorium of the Lyric Theatre to leave the upper tier in darkness to create a sense of intimacy when it is not needed. Because of the range of activities, we also wanted a variable acoustic. The required opera reverberation times would have

 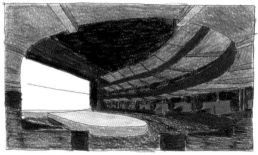

produced a tall vertical room, and I thought we must have an architectural ceiling to cap the space and ensure an appropriate intimate scale. We made the architectural ceiling acoustically transparent. The centre of the ceiling is a stainless-steel grid that is illuminated when the audience enters the room. The theatre lights are above it and shine through it during performances. The perimeter of the ceiling consists of a series of over-lapping panels of perforated metal. This arrangement allows adjustable acoustics within an architecturally contained space." To manipulate reverberation times, Wilford installed a series of adjustable curtains in boxes within the void above the architectural ceiling to dampen the acoustic and to absorb sound when required.

The smaller theatre is modelled on The Swan at Stratford-upon-Avon. In contrast to the soft finishes of the Lyric Theatre, the studio is given a rougher, workshop finish. The stage and upper seating balconies are the only fixed elements, and the seating on the main central floor can be reconfigured to create a thrust, promenade or end-stage (proscenium arch) configuration.

Wilford is the kind of architect who carries a clear idea of the end result he wants to achieve in his mind. Drawings are an important tool for working through those ideas. *"We don't do 100 options, the objective is clear, and then there are adjustments of the details, not the fundamentals."*

The transparent quality of The Lowry at night is one of its key characteristics. From the plaza or the footbridge it is possible to see the bustling foyers and the intense light of the canopy, which turns, as day dies into night, from solid to diaphanous form.

Previous pages: **Detail of the Lyric Theatre; the thrust of the graceful lines of the balconies creates an intimacy both within the audience and between audience and performer. A vast space is made surprisingly private.**

"It has a chameleon quality that makes it feel good on even the dullest days"

For The Lowry's colour scheme he worked with paint-makers at ICI to explore a special range of colours, and their impact on one another. *"They painted 8 x 4 sheets of plasterboard and lined them up for me so that we could ensure that the colour steps were discernible but subtle."*

The colour in the Lyric Theatre starts as a strong blue and goes gently through to purple, near the proscenium; the colour is brightest at the back wall. In the smaller theatre, colours shift from rust to bright red.

The Lowry is a key piece of architecture for Salford, and no less so for Wilford, marking the transition in his career from working in partnership to leading his own firm. As a phenomenon it clearly invites comparison with other high-profile, culturally led regeneration programmes such as the Guggenheim in Bilbao. But The Lowry has a distinctive voice of its own. It is designed for its site, and for its own unique mix of activities. Above all it is the culmination of Wilford's lifelong fascination for the way that we move in and around buildings.

Michael Wilford dedicates this publication to
Felicity Goodey, Chairman of the Lowry Trust, whose
vision and tenacity made the building what it is.

Acknowledgments are due to the following:

Architect
Michael Wilford & Partners, Limited
Michael Wilford, Russell Bevington, Laurence Bain
Associates: Stuart McKnight and Simon Usher

Project Managers
Gleeds Management Services

Structural, Mechanical & Electrical Services Engineer
Buro Happold

Quantity Surveyors
Davis Langdon & Everest

Theatre Consultant
Theatre Project Consultants

Acoustic Consultant
Sandy Brown Associates

Gallery Consultant
Lord Cultural Resources

Publishing and editorial direction by Roger Sears
Edited by Michael Leitch
Designed by Martin Tilley at Pocknell Studio

Published by The Lowry Press
The Lowry
Pier 8
Salford Quays
Salford M5 2AZ
Telephone: 44 (0) 161 876 2020
Fax: 44 (0) 161 876 2021
www.thelowry.com

First published 2001
© The Lowry Centre Limited
Text © Deyan Sudjic
All images © Arcaid
Richard Bryant / www.arcaid.co.uk

A CIP catalogue record for this book is available from The British Library
ISBN 1 902970 10 1
Originated, printed and bound in UK by The Good News Press

The Lowry Project has received support from the National Lottery
through the Arts Council of England, the Millennium Commission and
the Heritage Lottery Fund and from the European Regional Development
Fund, English Partnerships, North West Water, the City of Salford and
the former Trafford Park Development Corporation.

The Lowry in sunshine, seen from the south across the Manchester Ship Canal.

The Lowry and its plaza, designed as an outdoor performance space.

The Lowry: Architects Michael Wilford & Partners Ltd / Photograph © Arcaid

↻ **The Lowry: the sculptural shapes create a surreal urban landscape.**

The Lowry: Architects Michael Wilford & Partners Ltd / Photograph © Arcaid

The Lowry as seen from the Imperial War Museum: North.

The Lowry: Architects Michael Wilford & Partners Ltd / Photograph © Arcaid

◓ **The Lowry at night showing the entrance and foyer.**

The Lowry: Architects Michael Wilford & Partners Ltd / Photograph © Arcaid

↻ **The Lowry: detail of the junction between the Quays Theatre and the ArtWorks Gallery.**

The Lowry: Architects Michael Wilford & Partners Ltd / Photograph © Arcaid

The Lowry at dusk.

The Lowry: Architects Michael Wilford & Partners Ltd / Photograph © Arcaid

The Lowry: the beautiful sweeping lines of the Lyric Theatre.

The Lowry: Architects Michael Wilford & Partners Ltd / Photograph © Arcaid